Let's Read About Our Bodies

Mouth

By Cynthia Klingel and Robert B. Noyed

Reading consultant: Cecilia Minden-Cupp, Ph.D.,
Adjunct Professor, College of Continuing and Professional Studies, University of Virginia

Gareth Stevens
Publishing

Please visit our Web site www.garethstevens.com. For a free color catalog of all our high-quality books, call toll free 1-800-542-2595 or fax 1-877-542-2596.

Library of Congress Cataloging-in-Publication Data

Klingel, Cynthia.
Mouth / by Cynthia Klingel and Robert B. Noyed.
p. cm. – (Let's read about our bodies)
Includes bibliographical references and index.
Summary: An introduction to the mouth, what it is used for, and how to take care of it.
ISBN: 978-1-4339-3368-4 (lib. bdg.)
ISBN: 978-1-4339-3369-1 (pbk.)
ISBN: 978-1-4339-3370-7 (6-pack)
1. Mouth–Juvenile literature. [1. Mouth.]
I. Noyed, Robert B. II. Title.
QM306.K553 2002
611'.31–dc21 2001055053

New edition published 2010 by
Gareth Stevens Publishing
111 East 14th Street, Suite 349
New York, NY 10003

Original edition published 2003 by Weekly Reader® Books
An imprint of Gareth Stevens Publishing

Art direction: Haley Harasymiw, Tammy Gruenewald
Page layout: Daniel Hosek, Katherine A. Goedheer
Editorial direction: Kerri O'Donnell, Diane Laska Swanke

Photo credits: Cover, pp. 11, 19 shutterstock.com; pp. 5, 7, 9, 13, 15, 17, 21 Gregg Andersen.

Printed in the United States of America

CPSIA compliance information: Batch #WW10GS: For further information contact Gareth Stevens, New York, New York at 1-800-542-2595.

Table of Contents

Boldface words appear in the glossary.

My Mouth

This is my mouth.

I use my mouth
to eat.

I use my mouth
to talk.

I use my mouth
to sing.

We use our mouths to smile.

A Healthy Mouth

I have **teeth** in my mouth. I brush them every morning and every night.

I take care of my mouth. I go to the **dentist**.

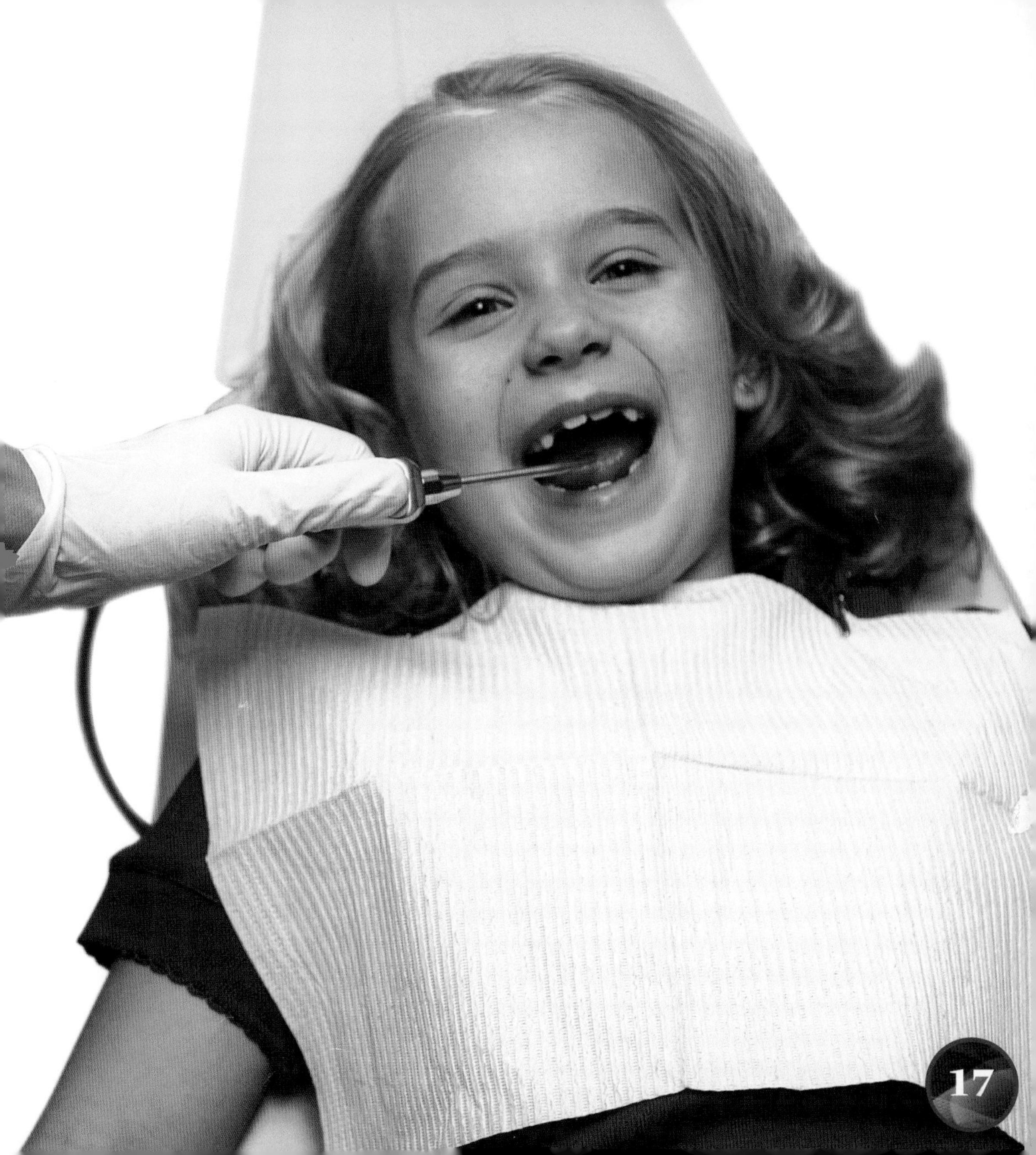

The dentist helps keep my teeth clean and **healthy**.

We make funny faces with our mouths!

Glossary

dentist: a doctor who cares for the teeth and mouth

healthy: good for the body

teeth: the hard, bony parts of the mouth used to bite and chew

For More Information

Books

Civardi, Anne. *Going to the Dentist*. Eveleth, MN: Usborne Books, 2005.

Douglas, Lloyd G. *My Mouth*. New York: Children's Press, 2004.

Larranaga, Ana Martin. *The Big Wide-Mouthed Frog*. London: Walker Books, 2003.

Nunn, Daniel. *Mouths*. Chicago: Heinemann-Raintree, 2007.

Web Sites

What Is Spit?

kidshealth.org/kid/talk/yucky/spit.html

To learn why we have saliva in our mouths

Publisher's note to educators and parents: Our editors have carefully reviewed these Web sites to ensure that they are suitable for students. Many Web sites change frequently, however, and we cannot guarantee that a site's future contents will continue to meet our high standards of quality and educational value. Be advised that students should be closely supervised whenever they access the Internet.

Index

About the Authors

Cynthia Klingel has worked as a high school English teacher and an elementary school teacher. She is currently the curriculum director for a Minnesota school district. Cynthia Klingel lives with her family in Mankato, Minnesota.

Robert B. Noyed started his career as a newspaper reporter. Since then, he has worked in school communications and public relations at the state and national level. Robert B. Noyed lives with his family in Brooklyn Center, Minnesota.